Praise / *Details of*

D0390730

Like her concept of nursing, Cortney Davis's poems are "fierce" and "physical" and—I would add—brilliant. She doesn't look away from anything that is human: our textures, oozings, and dreams when we are wounded, or our ghastly beauty as we are dying.
—Joanne Trautmann Banks,
founding editor of *Literature and Medicine*

Scenes in Cortney Davis's poems—in the hospital, in the shower, on the road—are drawn with sure strokes and precise, evocative detail; they unfold at a suspenseful pace. Her language—whether it is medical terminology of a pelvic examination or erotic language of mother love—moves on sustained music. Like a nurse, though many of the poems are not about nursing, she imagines the unimaginable—children burned in a fire, carnage of the Vietnam war—with a clear eye. She does not draw back, remains efficient, records the telling and humanizing details. Like nurses, we are able to see more than we might have wanted to and to open our eyes with wonder, not turn away. In her amazing poems, Cortney Davis takes us into new territory. We are in good hands. —Sondra Zeidenstein, poet, editor,
and publisher, Chicory Blue Press

[Cortney Davis's] nursing experience informs in a deeper sense her understanding of the body—its physical needs and pain, and the other forms of human suffering these can give rise to. In the recent burgeoning of medical poetry by medical caregivers, this collection is truly outstanding for the author's keen sensitivity to the nuances of sound, word, and image. Cortney Davis is indeed a gifted poet.
—Anne Hunsaker Hawkins, author of *Archetypes of Conversion*
and *Reconstructing Illness: Studies in Pathography*

What sets Cortney Davis's exceptional first full collection of poems apart from others is not only its stress-insistent craft—words and phrases, rhythms and details set down with absolute fidelity to real events—but its unique describing of how the mind whirls from the body. "I sensed the potential in disorder," Davis writes in "Blood Clot," and in "Night Nurse" the nurse-Angel is "the one who gentles the world"; it is she who cherishes "all these lives flying from us." Details of Flesh is a book of narratives and rhapsodies of caring—personal but not confessional— from a shocking and sensual poet who inhabits the body of an accomplished and professional woman.
—Dick Allen, author of *Ode to the Cold War: Poems New and Selected*

Details of Flesh

Details of Flesh

NOV 1997

for Michele —
    sister nurse —

enjoy these poems about our
work!
        Cortney Davis

Cortney Davis

CALYX Books   Corvallis Oregon

The publication of this book was supported in part with grants from the Oregon Arts Commission, the Lannan Foundation, and the Meyer Memorial Trust.

With grateful appreciation, CALYX acknowledges the following "Immortals" who provided substantial support for this book:

Nancy S. Nordhoff

The Woodard Family Foundation

Beta Anderson

The Microsoft Corporation

Cover art "The Face" by Shelly Corbett
Cover and book design by Cheryl McLean

CALYX Books are distributed to the trade through **Consortium Book Sales and Distribution, Inc., St. Paul, MN, 1-800-283-3572.**

CALYX Books are also available through major library distributors, jobbers, and most small press distributors including: Airlift, Baker & Taylor, Banyan Tree, Bookpeople, Ingram, and Small Press Distribution. For personal orders or other information write: CALYX Books, PO Box B, Corvallis, OR 97339, (541) 753-9384, FAX (541) 753-0515.

∞

The paper in this book meets the guidelines for permanence and durability of the Committee on Production Guidelines for Book Longevity of the Council on Library Resources and the minimum requirements of the American National Standard for the Permanence of Paper for Printed Library Materials Z38.48-1984.

Library of Congress Cataloging-in-Publication Data
Davis, Cortney,
        Details of Flesh / Cortney Davis.
             p. cm.
        ISBN 0-934971-58-7 (hc : alk. paper) : $23.95 —ISBN
        0-934971-57-9 (pb : alk. paper) : $11.95
             1. Caregivers—Poetry. I. Title.
        PS3554.A93342D48 1997
        811'.54—dc21   97-6686
                                                                     CIP

Printed in the U.S.A.
9 8 7 6 5 4 3 2 1

Acknowledgments

Grateful acknowledgment is given to the editors of the following publications in which these poems listed first appeared, some in slightly different versions: *CALYX Journal:* "The Smoke We Make Pictures Of"; *Connecticut River Review:* "The Good Nurse"; *Crazyhorse:* "Hemorrhage, 3 A.M.," "On the Wards," "How I Imagine It"; *The Hudson Review:* "The Barking Dog," "The Body Flute"; *The International Journal of Arts Medicine:* "The Nurse's Task" © 1991 MMB Music, Inc., Saint Louis, used by permission, all rights reserved; *Jack the Daw:* "Tumor Board"; *The Journal of Medical Humanities:* "Old Lady Patient," "Slow Code"; *Kaleidoscope:* "To the Mother of the Burned Children"; *Literature and Medicine:* "Doctor, 8 P.M.," reprinted by permission of the Johns Hopkins University Press; *Ms.:* "Patient, 7 A.M."; *Poet & Critic:* "Duet," "The Woman Who Lost Her Breast to Cancer and Said She Didn't Mind"; *Poetry East:* "Details of Flesh"; *Poets On:* "Ritual Bath, 1955"; *Second Glance:* "Visiting My Father in the Hospital"; *Slow Dancer:* "Blood Clot"; *Sojourner:* "On Not Loving Your Children," "What Man Might Kill," "Nurse, 7 A.M."; *Viet Nam Generation:* "Flashback"; *Yankee:* "Old Men Name the Planets."

"What the Nurse Likes," "Night Nurse," "Becoming the Patient," and sections 1, 2, and 5 of "Suffering" first appeared in *The Body Flute* (Adastra Press, 1994). "This Happened" first appeared in *Between the Heartbeats: Poetry and Prose by Nurses* (University of Iowa Press, 1995). "To the Husband Who Stands at the Sink, Intent on Shaving" first appeared in *Grow Old Along With Me, The Best Is Yet To Be* (Papier-Mache Press, 1996).

Excerpts from "Osip Mandelstam: 394" translated with Anne Frydman from *THE MESSENGER* by Jean Valentine. Copyright © 1979 by Jean Valentine. Reprinted by permission of Farrar, Strauss & Giroux, Inc.

My gratitude to The National Endowment for the Arts and the Connecticut Commission on the Arts for grants that provided time to write. Very special thanks to Dick Allen, Honor Moore, and Sondra Zeidenstein, and also to Irene Sherlock, Mark Fadiman, Gary Metras, E.J. Miller Laino, Jean Sands, and my husband, Jonathan Gordon.

For my children,
Lisa and Christopher

Contents

III. *The Body Flute*

There are women,
the damp earth's flesh and blood:
every step they take, a cry,
a deep steel drum.

It is their calling
to accompany those who have died;
and to be there, the first
to greet the resurrected.

To ask for their tenderness
would be a trespass against them;
but to go off, away from them—
no one has the strength.

Today an angel; tomorrow
worms, and the grave;
and the days after
only lines in chalk

—from Mandelstam's #394
translated by Jean Valentine
with Anne Frydman

I.

What Man Might Kill

Staring into the Point Where the Tracks Merge

I am staring down the tracks
as if staring would bring the train,
as if staring would bring anything.
There is a long time for thinking
and something time does to thoughts—
compresses them, the rain and the moon
half-seen behind trees, a row of them
like silent women.

A man with a daughter joins me.
We all stand staring into the point
where the tracks merge.
We move our feet on the damp platform
watching our footprints appear,
lighten, and go back into wood.
I wonder about the man and his daughter.
Maybe someday he will fall in love

with a woman who is not her mother,
becoming hateful even to himself.
For now he is afraid that his child
stands too close, and he calls her back.
Then there is a silent time
when he thinks she is safe, and we wait,
satisfied with blue air
and the grace of tree limbs that rise
like women's hair into evening.

The Smoke We Make Pictures Of

Wrapping presents, I look up
and see the clock in the mirror,
how it seems to tick backwards.

In the living room, gifts unwrap,
ribbons recoil on their spools;
my life peels like a time-lapse flower.

I haven't yet met you.
My first marriage falls apart,
my children's legs telescope into their bodies

and they scamper away, curl
like the ends of unused ribbon.
I feel them drawn into me; my water,

splashed at the doctor's shoes, gathers
and the sack seals. For a moment
I think we could start again,

but the hands click back,
the cells of my tiny children shrink
into droplets. Sperm swim, frantic,

and disappear into my husband.
I am free. My hair grows long,
I'm in college throwing water balloons—

they explode, spray rises
and settles like sequins.
Now I'm in my yard in Pittsburgh,

the sprinkler waves a shimmering barrier,
my bare feet print the grass.
Father, just balding, still drinking,

laughs and lights a cigarette.
Mother, tall and pretty in her housedress,
her dark glasses black as night,

comes out with Zipper. He wags his tail
and smacks his jaws at the mist falling.
I'm so happy I want to stop the hands,

but they inch back and I'm three, sitting
by the mantle, father snapping a Kodak
as I frown up, waiting for Santa.

I don't know that mother's just home
from the doctor, her lung cradling
its dark spot, returned from the jar

where it will rest thirty years later.
Father's breath is tinged with Four Roses,
his arms with their spotty freckles

rewind the film, undoing the knot of cancer
drifting in his colon, scattering the pages
of the novel he knows he can write,

but never will. Then I spiral into myself,
we all disappear into mother's angular hips.
Her uterus bulges under the hot fuchsia skirt

my father loved. It's the weekend he was home
on leave. As they lie pressed together,
he takes back that part of me he will love most:

the way I draw horses with manes flying up
like blackbirds, frightened, rising in unison.
The way I let him stroke my long fingers

late at night, while mother waits upstairs.
With the final gasp of their union,
I am gone.

Father reaches for a match.
They talk about how I'll be theirs someday,
and they watch the clock on the bureau

tick, each of them exhaling smoke into air,
clouds they make pictures of. A house
at Christmas. A dog. A little girl.

Blood Clot

I got sleepy, my right side
became lazy, then wouldn't move.
Inside my lids a plush curtain
turned my friend's rosy face
into a ripe tomato. Mother's
purple violets against the porcelain
kitchen sink became that thick pulse
stopped in my brain. At twelve
I never wanted to be a nurse,
but head down on my arms at the table,

I sensed the potential in disorder.
My friend chattered to keep me awake
while father phoned the doctor.
When he said *Emergency*, dad opened
a can of Campbell's Bean and Bacon soup,
stirred it slowly in mom's enamel pan.
Keep talking, he told my friend,
while I obediently spooned,
with my good left hand, the dusty aftertaste
of soup he'd make me finish first,

when all I wanted were alarms,
women in white bright enough to burn
running with me in their arms.
When at last I was delivered
to their headlong rush, their quick
needle in my vein, their silent
bedside vigil I could count on, I vowed
I would always love their way: Fierce.
Physical. Then they returned me, healed,
to that damn, calm kitchen.

Ritual Bath, 1955

Steam-laden air and the summer night's heat
met and rose over us, mother and I adrift
on that Saturday night in Pittsburgh.
Ivory soap globes burst with a small

sting and ping, like seconds ticked away
by the Baby Ben on her bedside stand.
We bathed without speaking.
My fingerpads became old. Her breasts

rested sleepy on the meniscus of the water;
flakes of our skin made a ring
on the surface. The cloth was rough.
Heat lightning from a distant town

flared in the high bathroom window,
and the slippery curve of mother
rounded into pale fuchsia nipples
color of lips, of tongues, of the damask

rose towel slung on the door hook.
I gathered armfuls of soapsuds,
prisms that held mother's many faces
shimmering like fish roe—faces released

like a handful of new, glittering fish.
She plucked the stopper.
The water, sluicing down the dark
hatched mouth, left soap-foam clinging

to my chest, my own erect goosebumps.
Mother, suddenly cold, shivered and rose
from the boil of heat, a woman
rushing to her damask towel.

On Not Loving Your Children

Stop loving them at two.
August nights, when rain comes in the window
and lightning snaps the air,
don't run to them.
Or, if you must, don't look in their eyes,
the clear glass of your own fear.

If you love them at ten,
turn away from baseball, dance class,
or the riding ring. Their slim bodies
split the air like fish.

By sixteen there is no hope.
They circle farther and farther away,
whistling to friends in strange tongues,
shining in skin you don't remember
touching or bathing.

At twenty, they are gone,
the air filled with their mist.
If you love them still, turn on your back,
stare into the sun for their reflections,
swirling and leaping like burning gases,
the sea-swell, the undertow.

Old Men Name the Planets

Old men name the planets and their moons;
seeing birds at the feeder
they watch the empty seed pods fall
like shooting stars.

My father writes copy in his mind at night.
Sleepless, he edits, sets the type,
goes to press. By morning
his words are ghosts in the sky.

I've begun to read the weather.
Today named rain before the thunder,
called the time and duration,
knew which way to turn my back

against the wind. Already,
I feel it going. Soon I too
will search for words:
nimbus   stratus   cumulus—

summers from remembered summers,
the smell in the air before snow.
Snowballs in my children's hands
will be white and distant as the moon.

What Man Might Kill

*On November 29, 1988, Susan Galvin and
Martha Alsup were brutally murdered
on a remote beach on the island of Anguilla.
They were two women traveling alone. . . .*
                                    —Sojourner

1.

He lights a cigarette
begged from the sheriff who kept them

from lynching him, *hanging your crazy ass,
you understand?* He nods, and his fear

is a pocketful of stones.
When he was a boy he took his father's canoe,

dragged it over coarse shells to the beach
where sand turned smooth as skin. He slid his legs

into the wooden hatch and paddled out
like a small man wedged inside another man.

He became a dot bobbing on the horizon
under a seabird's distant ellipse;

he paddled until he thought he'd drown.
Then he turned to see his island

indifferent as a woman sleeping,
her arms up over her head

toward Captain's Point, sun blinding him
as if she'd forgotten a mirror by her side.

2.

On Sundays, the voices of women
circled him like seabirds,
and the sea in the curved harbor
hissed and tumbled back, not like
children playing but like firesmoke rolling.
His eyes were black as the grackles
that pecked nits from goats
grazing in the churchyard. And no half-moon

showed below his iris. His mother
was glad, believing that white sliver,
like a pared fingernail,
meant death. He sang in the choir,
in the blue peeling churches,
but he felt death in the quiet sheath of water
that sealed over his body, in the way
the salt dried and pinched his skin.

3.

Finally, it was the women on the beach.
He watched them through vines of seagrape
as he plucked the ripe berries.
He saw how they considered each other,
how they drew one-finger paths
through sand crusting the other's skin.
They were overcome with a rapture

he'd seen women give in to at church:
the presence of something holy
on the salt-skim of their lips,
how one woman spoke the prayer of another
with the curve of her tongue. The sun rose
in bright lines over the ends of the world.
He went crazy, the cops said later.

4.

Through the window slit of his cell,
the low scrub of island disappears at nightfall
and the sea pinpoints beneath the moon
like confetti scattering.

Under the tide, the sand is stone
and shell crushed a million years,
anything living relentlessly knit
into the firm white matrix of silica

and otolith. His cigarette ash falls.
There is a sound in the dark, the entrance
of a cormorant into water, the bucket-mouth
scooping a fish that couldn't turn away,

just risen from beneath the breakers
having seen the moon.

Flashback

All these acts are intended to deaden the heart.
—Susan Griffin

Fuck yourself with a bottle;
take down your panties and tease me.
If I refused he'd fast forward

a porno film to the good part—
the woman being sandwiched by two men.
He said to get hard he thought

of girlfriends who married someone else
or the girls in Vietnam who liked
butterfly kisses after sex,

his eyelashes beating their fragile bodies.
Every night he got stoned, slowing
the visions: His own men falling

from the white decks, shirts
and backs torn open, sparking.
His men pitching dimes to children

who dove for coins in the Perfume River,
tossing them the shiny grenade
they fished up like a prize

a second before the puff of smoke,
the hole blown in the surface
through which water snakes slid,

like fingers, to clutch the banks.
Drunk one night, he and the men
fired at a line of children,

at the mothers keening their grief-cries,
at the barefoot husbands waiting behind them,
bayonets fixed. He showed me

how he stood then, tore
away his shirt, pointed to his heart—
asking for it. Begging.

Visiting My Father
in the Hospital

Where the tongue on the palate
finds softness, there
before the uvula,
my father has a tumor.
I watch while he sleeps—
snow ticks against the window;

a nurse strokes his hollow lips.
Temperature at four,
juice at eight, backrub
and pills at ten.
No one asks for more
where elevators hold death.

My father wakes
as nurses whisper past.
He touches their linen sleeves.
My pain, he says, *my pain*.

I want to tell him, beware—
nurses are whores, ashes
under their fingernails.
Instead I say: Break the window.
Let your tongue melt snow.
When you leave, take the stairs.

Suffering

1.

Jean tells me about her heart scan—
a shiny isotope failed to light up
the scarred tip of her ventricle.

Another friend's mother dies
finally at sixty-five pounds.
In Lithuania she had been a dentist
smiling from old black-and-white photos;
in America she raised chickens
and learned to cook.

I dream Jean dies too.

Waking, I realize it isn't death I fear
but that half-death, suffering,
so I can barely speak
of the patients kept alive:

> The eighty-five-year-old farmer, ribs cracked,
> all of them, to get his heart going,
> or the burned woman whose arteries
> we pierced through the crust of her skin.

2.

In intensive care,
these sufferings:

a baby whose father had taken him
by both legs, a finger between them,

and hit the baby against the wall
because the baby cried. With the other hand

he held the mother back. A boy
who fell off his bike and was hit by a car.

His mother watched him lying
in the clean sheets, his heart

beating under his chest
as if an animal were trying to escape.

The monitor line straightened;
then she howled for him.

There was a child who drowned
and a crazy woman we tied to the mattress

who rose up
with the mattress still on her back.

Once a man ran naked down the back stairs
into the parking lot

just to feel for the last time
the hard diamonds of snow.

3.

I've seen women
who were beaten

by other women
with a shoe, a stick, a picture frame.

A mother hits
the side of her daughter's face
with a flashlight.

Fathers use their hands,
to women mostly,
to their children
maybe something else.

One woman told me it wasn't the blows
but the love lost,
gone as if they peeled your skin,
sucked all marrow from your bones and now
you walk everywhere hollow.

4.

It was January.

We met friends in New York City
at the Drake Hotel.

Every time the door opened
we saw a woman and her child
humped under their blanket
lying over a subway grate—
the great curve
of mother around child.

As I sucked pimento
from the olive,
salty clam
from mother-of-pearl,
I imagined them
sleeping
there outside 440 Park.

I finished everything
on my plate. I had dessert
and walked away with the others
scattering to cars
or calling taxis with our smoke-words,
fingering the linings of our coats,
bundling deeper into our coats.

5.

Here is Lisa Steinberg in 1987,
her old face with its straight brows,

the window behind her like the window
of Washington School

where children's drawings, one of them mine,
were clipped by clothespins to a string.

Lisa half-rises from her chair,
looking at someone

we can't see, saying something
no one hears.

6.

This is their sound.

It starts as a whine,
like children whine
when they can't have
what they want;

then it becomes
mindless,
a staccato rap
finding your pulse;

then
intermittent,

like the high sound
when intestines churn,
trying to find something left
to pass through;

then it becomes
all there is,
small and pure,
a delicious drop
balanced on the tongue
of the open mouth;

then,

Silence.

II.
The Nurse's Task

What the Nurse Likes

I like looking into patients' ears
and seeing what they can never see.

It's like owning them.

I like patients' honesty—
they trust me with simple things:
> They wake at night and count heartbeats.
> They search for lumps.

I am also afraid.

✪

I like the way women look at me
and feel safe.
Then I lean across them
and they smell my perfume.

I like the way men become shy.
Even angry men bow their heads
when they are naked.

✪

I like lifting a woman's hair
to place stethoscope to skin,
the way everyone breathes differently—

the way men make suggestive groans
when I listen to their hearts.

I like eccentric patients:
Old women who wear purple knit hats
and black eyeliner. Men
who put makeup over their age spots.

✪

I like talking about patients
as if they aren't real, calling them
"the fracture" or "the hysterectomy."

It makes illness seem trivial.

I like saying
> *You shouldn't smoke!*
> *You must have this test!*

I like that patients don't always
do what I say.

⊕

I like the way we stop the blood,
pump the lungs,
turn hearts off and on with electricity.

I don't like when it's over
and I realize

I know nothing.

⊕

I like being the one to give bad news;
I am not embarrassed by grief.

I like the way patients gather their hearts,
their bones, their arms and legs
that have spun away momentarily.

At the end of the gathering they sigh
and look up.

⊕

I like how dying patients become beautiful.

Their eyes concentrate light. Their skin
becomes thin and delicate as fog.
Nothing matters anymore
but sheets, pain, a radio, the time of day.

☩

I like watching patients die.

First they are living,
then something comes up from within
and moves from them.

They become vacant and yet
their bodies are heavy
and sink into the sheets.

I like how emptiness is seen first
in the eyes, then in the hands.

☩

I like taking care of patients
and I like forgetting them,

going home and sitting on my porch
while they stand away from me
talking among themselves.

I like how they look back
when I turn their way.

Nurse, 7 A.M.

She squints, eight hours
rising before her like bile.

Even when sleet clots her windshield
she drives on, thinking of grocery lists

or letters to write, to keep away
one more hour the man with bedsores

big as sinkholes. When lights turn
yellow, she waits—her husband at home

still snoring, big-boned, paws
like baseball mitts her mind smacks into.

Wheeling into the lot,
she crams thoughts, like hair, under her cap,

enters the whoosh of pneumatic doors,
forgetting the time her husband

took another woman, the time her father
touched her when her mother's back was turned.

That night she dreams her patients die,
her husband's hands puff up with gangrene

and burst, the sun comes out screaming
like a newborn, round and lemon.

The Nurse's Task

When I pluck the suture
or pack the ulcer with gauze,
it becomes my task
to introduce rage to this body

that calls me *nurse, nurse,*
as if my hands were gold.
I cradle the body
like a mother rocks.

I lean close
and let it memorize my face.
Then, I begin.
First, something subtle.

A hasty scrape.
An accidental pinch
as if I might thrust needle
down to bone. The body

raises its hands in disbelief!
This is nothing. I thread veins
with catheters of fire,
I change morphine to milk.

When the body asks *why*?
I am silent. When the body
whines, I act bored
and turn away. If sleep comes

I sneak in and shake the body
until, angry and squinty-eyed,
it rises on its elbow
and stares at me, at last understanding

that the flesh is everything.
This is the body I love—the one
that laughs down death's trumpet.
The one that escapes.

This Happened

> *My point is that illness*
> *is* not *a metaphor.*
> —Susan Sontag

The intern and I begin our rounds.
In room two, the intern watches me;
he doesn't like this patient anyway—

she's messy, a see-through plastic tube
pulls bile from her stomach
to a bottle near her head.

A small balloon inside her throat
keeps pressure
on vessels wrecked by years of gin.

The patient's wide awake,
but she can't talk.
I see her eyes open, her skin

pale at the moment these veins
blow, like a tire blows.
Blood backs up her nose.

She tries to sit;
her wrists are tied.
I take her hand and say *OK. OK.*

The intern leaves.
Next, the patient's gut lets go.
Stool and blood clot between her legs,

hot and soft, not like sex,
more like giving birth. *OK,* I say.
We let our fingers intertwine.

By 8:15 the woman calms.
Clots thicken in her throat;
she holds her breath.

At nine, blood coins
close her eyes. I breathe deep,
stroke the patient's arm.

The intern,
who went downstairs to sleep,
will ask me later.

But what happened here
can't be said again
and be the same.

Patient in Surgery, 7 A.M.

Dazed by the needle's punch,
she sees faces ooze into spotlights,
the staff, hooded and slow,
bent to their task like aliens.

She never knows
if she's awake or sleeping—
only that her mind swells,
a merry-go-round begins
and she rides the rise and fall
of black rubber and stainless steel.

They told her she wouldn't dream,
but she runs naked in the body of her youth
while men shout some foreign language
she forgets at once. She wakes
screaming with her mouth shut.

She raised six kids, had a man once
whose body cleaved hers
like a blade splits an apple.
When he left, she wore her knees down
scrubbing other women's floors.

New sutures draw the edges
of her wounds tight; she wonders
how long silk can hold. Later
she tells everyone how the knife
went in before she was ready.

The Woman Who Lost Her Breast to Cancer and Said She Didn't Mind

Because she could still reach her arm
over her head, walking her fingers up the wall
doing *itsy-bitsy spider* in her mind.

Because the scar wasn't as ugly as she'd heard,
only a burnt sienna slash with a single
pink bulge of flesh that somehow was puckered
by sutures, like smocking on an apron
you couldn't take off.

Because the fluid that drained
from the lymph system's tangle of vessels
caused the pocket of flesh to swell,
resembling a single stunted breast,
but usually seeped out by morning.

Because the cancer didn't invade her lymph nodes
and the CAT scan of her brain was clear,
so she took hormones instead of poisons
and she didn't lose her hair,
but her chin whiskers grew like a billy goat's.

Really because she had no man anymore,
no husband or boyfriend, and without a man
who needs these things hanging down,
they just get in your way. She pushes

her sweater over the flat spot, the desert,
unzips her dress, *Wanna see?*

I see her words ooze from her chest,
their wounded red hearts,
their own nightmare chests pared clean
as beef shanks in the cooler.
That night, alone in my bed,
I cradle my breasts, blue-veined
beautiful fruits, thin rosy teats
that might suckle the world, and say
mine   mine.

Duet

We sing her down on the table, slowly.
Then we help as she rocks her hips
to the edge, where the table falls away
like the falling away of her breath
when the man entered her, the young man
she'd let stroke her thigh, like I do now,

getting her used to my touch.
Then the speculum. Warm, unwieldy,
its mouth clamped, I guide it carefully,
part the dark tangle and the sweet
glistening walls that echo
the musty smell of lust. She moves

and the nurse caresses her arm.
I rise into the chorus of curves
and vestibules, peering into the never-opened
cervical os, the small bulb not yet tinged
with the blue stain of her pregnancy.
She readies herself for what comes next.

With one hand inside, the other
on her belly, rolling and kneading the organs
between, the lining thickened and ripe,
I rock the boggy womb.
Her breasts thrust up
beneath the paper drape; her thin labia

glitter with the clear slippery stuff
stirred by my finger's dance.
She's silent and cold, wishing
this small whine inside would either drop dead
or swell to a fine refrain
that would crack the dome of her fear.

Abortion

All the women cry,
their legs slung over metal cradles
in these small white rooms.

Nurses hold their hands.
Later the nurses say
I knew she'd do fine or

I knew she'd throw up.
Between cases the doctor waits,
eating a sandwich.

When the nurse calls,
the doctor caps his Pepsi.
He numbs the cervix,

grasps it with a clamp.
He dilates the os with metal probes,
each bigger than the one before.

I feel sick! the women say
when the suction
gurgles.

They hear
instruments clink; the doctor
packs their vaginas with gauze.

The suction is rolled away.
White leggings peel
from the women's calves

like borrowed skin.
A nurse finds Streisand
on the radio. The women

stop crying.
If they have children,
they show each other pictures.

I Hear the Cries of Women

Women in the clinic waiting room
women from the shelter
women who live on the hill
girls from the city
girls from out of town
any girl, any woman
any man ever had
because she was patient
had no other place to go
wanted to please
wanted to be whole
had no choice
couldn't speak
wasn't heard.

There's the woman
who can't take the pill.
It makes her pressure go up
it makes her vomit
it makes migraines grind her brain
like chain saws
it makes her fat and crazy.
Her man doesn't like fat
(really hates crazy)
but he won't wear condoms
the diaphragm
chafed him, foam
turned his dick red.
She tells him, honey
I'm pregnant
and he says
liar, it can't be mine.

There's the child just thirteen
who learned everything she knows
from Mr. Seventeen:

you can't get pregnant the first time
you won't if you don't come
you can't if I don't come inside
you won't if you stand up right after
you won't if you douche
you won't if you do it when you bleed.

She found out he was wrong
on at least one count
now her mother tells her
don't bring any piece of trash
you deliver
home to me.

A girl calls
her boyfriend. He said
if you love me you'll have my baby.
His line is ringing
she's still holding.

A woman says
     This is killing me.

She's on the exam table
she has one fist raised.

She says
     I can't I won't

her fist punctuates
     bring another child
     into this world.

Hemorrhage, 3 A.M.

A boy walks into the sea.
Content at first, he floats
in the trivial current,
paddles like a dog.
Drifting, he streams
through a cold spot. His legs
cool, his arm hairs stand up
making him laugh.
Now he's moving.

White caps peak and dip.
He thinks he could swim to shore
like a hero.

If he stops, his arms and legs
splay out and he's pulled along.
When the sea rocks, he rocks,
one with the onward rush.

Now he's moving.

He tries to speak and blood
tongues his throat.
He remembers how mother lifted him
from the tub, enclosed him in a towel.
He thinks of smacking baseballs
with a wooden bat.

When he goes under
his hair circles and he sees it
as if he is above himself.
He's a boy-fish

moving with the tide
like a bullet, like a shark.

He thinks he'll wash ashore
and eat the children.

His body elongates.
Gulls would mistake him
for a woman's scarf trailed from a boat
or a kite tail
looping in the wind.

Far off, children play
in bright suits. The beach
is crowded with mothers.

      He turns into a ripple,
            a crease in the surface of the sea.

To the Mother of
the Burned Children

When you ask, when your voice
is your own again, and you know
you're not waking from sleep
or a vision of kids napping,
the power gone, candles
shaking light across their faces,
I'll give it to you straight:
Your children are dead.

You can cry one long sound
and we'll let the bed quake,
the burned flesh fall away.
I could bring shots to lull you,
pills to stay your mourning,
but instead I'll tell you:
Walk the fire in your mind.
Carry them out, one by one,
through rooms thick with smoke.
Carry your children, then put them down
safe outside the ring of heat.

Call them by name:
Ramon. Priss. Jamal.

Tell them *Wait.*
Wait here. Wait.

Tumor Board

The woman has lost her vulva
to cancer. Now doctors gather
to discuss the pros and cons of method
as they view the remains.
The pull-down screen glistens;
someone kills the lights.

In the first slide, the specimen—
imagine the cunt of a woman in *Playboy*
cut from between her legs
and photographed. The edges pucker,
the mound drips iodine.

In a moment, you adjust:
clitoris, labia, sparse hair.
The surgeon stands,
his hand's shadow pointing
as they argue margin, technique,
the grace of a centimeter.

The next slide takes one slice
at a time down to cells,
purple stain of nuclei dividing,
comfort of membrane intact.
The woman is forgotten—
the injured vulva no longer her own,

the red slash between her legs
bandaged in white. But one man
is relentless. He takes his silver pointer,
bangs it against the screen,
the magnified cancer. "Here," he says,
banging. "Here and here and here."

Night Nurse

Angel,

hold their hands while I hurry
from patient to nameless patient,

feeling their skin beneath my hands
like tattered dresses stinking

of urine. Now they are sobbing.
Touch me! an old man says, *Touch me.*

The women want to steal my flesh.
They cry out *Take my place!*

Angel, you go. Go into the corridors
where their bodies wither before me.

They die rolling in their beds,
they die sitting on their toilets.

When I try to give them breath
their vomit comes into my mouth.

Angel,

when a patient's skin is moist with pain
and pain wakes him and sings him to sleep,

when a patient's family turns away
and his hands fall empty to the sheets,

then everything is multiplied.
A sip of cold water could be a thousand lakes;

a nurse appearing uncalled in the doorway
could be someone who loves him.

Angel, when their lungs stop and their eyes
slick over and stare, when their skin

purples from toe to thumb to hollow cheek,
you be the one who gentles the world;

you be the one who stays,
all these lives flying from us.

Details of Flesh

That morning I surprised a nurse
and her patient, the two of them
together, bloodless skin and white
uniform like a shroud, but her hair,

it was black and crackling.
Then the sunburned neurologist
stripped an unconscious girl.
Let's see if she responds.

He rolled her nipple hard
between his fingers. Her body
arched, her breasts amazed.
So later, when the new doctor

found me alone in the room,
my white uniform neon
under fluorescent tubes,
I said yes. His tongue was salty,

his hands cold. I tasted his skin
clammy with so many bodies,
and I thought of them, my washcloth
making their skin gather,

the stark light on the details
of flesh. That day, in every ward,
nurses dripped lotion into their cupped hands,
and restless patients called them.

Slow Code

Small room. Iron bed. Yellow sheets
that smell like bleach. Mrs. Gold's
stroked out, lived too long. Her son
wants no treatment spared.

Mrs. G. (we call her) curls in bed—
open-eyed, but no one's home.
We feed her—she chokes on juice.
When she wets, we put her diaper on.

We find her, warm,
still staring at the wall.
Our orders say Mrs. G's a "code."
The board is down the hall

so we drag her to the floor,
arrange her head,
and slowly pry
the airway in. No breath.

We hook Mrs. G. to oxygen
and fill her lungs. No pulse.
We measure between her breasts
and give a tap. Repeat. No pulse.

By now the team arrives.
How long she been out? the intern asks,
works his hands to pump her chest.
We shrug, say we'll check our notes

but don't. He cracks her ribs,
that slows him down.
Someone in the hall phones her son,
says things look bad.

Mrs. G. grunts each time
the intern's hands come down.
Her pupils star
to two black points, then flare.

Her face and arms are black and blue.
I think we've missed the boat,
the head nurse says. The intern
stops. *Did we ever get a pulse?*

We look. The ECG just shows
his effort's artificial spikes.
We shrug. We cover Mrs. Gold.
We'll tell her son *At least we tried.*

The Barking Dog

There is a woman
in a hospital
barking like a dog.
The nurses know
it's the sound
of her lungs going
and her heart.
Visitors think
it's a dog outside
chained to a tree,
the rope too short,
no water,
no one passing by.
All day and all night
visitors worry.
*Why doesn't someone
bring in that dog?*
People give the dog
names, people ask
if anyone can see the dog
through the window.
When the barking stops
everyone is relieved.
Elaborate endings are told—
how the dog
was taken to a farm
and set free.
How the dog
drinks from a stream
whenever it wants.
The nurses
say nothing.
But every nurse knows
the story
of the barking dog.

Old Lady Patient

I hate
doctors   they
do things to me
and nurses have
washrags of sand
they put their hands
down there, my face
is red just
saying it.
Water!
Bring me water!
Hah, my throat.
You look like
my daughter   nice
give me
your hand   cool like
water,   your name?

Becoming the Patient

1.

For years the same dream:

a pit beside the road, walls
made of dirt, women with matted hair
who called to me, their wails

sounding like lullabies.
I'm tired of being the nurse. I bend
close to the edge.

Will I be drawn into the patient
like thin wires of pain?

2.

First, the white gauze.

I probe the patient's wound;
its steep walls retract—
muscle and veins, their red glow

a lantern.
Voices come and go.
The hall lights dim. Then,

skin pressed to bone,
I enter the patient. My heart
becomes soft; its blood

echoes back unfamiliar places:
toes, temple, belly.

Who else knows what this is like?

3.

All day, my fever rages.
I see the nurses are crying,
eyes full of waiting, eyes
shiny as ice.

Beyond my window,
a field. The nurses sing to me.
They hold me
in the tall meadow grass.

I cannot turn from their bodies.

4.

My nurse smells cold as January.
Birds dart at her hair,
plucking for seeds in this long winter.
The birds see the window near my bed
and think it is air. One by one,
their soft bodies against it;
they have tried to go home for the night.
What is the point of being here?

5.

I open my eyes.
There is a moon in the hallway;
under it, nurses talk, their voices
like water traveling long viaducts.

When pirates with knives in their teeth
bend over me, I call my nurse.
She says *They don't want to kill you—
only to look.*

I close my eyes.

6.

The wound's edge has sucked shut.

My nurse tells me I am so good
I am free to go. After this,
nothing else is important.

I tell her my dream.
We have something in common, she says,
but she will forget me.

She says *It's time,*

7.

and everything is aflame.

Standing beside my patient,
I point out the thin scar.

III.

The Body Flute

Four Masks

The mask I see in the mirror:

A woman who has come to love silence,
who sees life through prisms, hexagonal
planes like the vision
of flying insects, so much color
breaking against reason. Thin
eyebrows. Nose off center.

The mask I wore for my mother:

Bright in the way of silk roses,
more than once it threw dinner
crashing to the floor and yet
was afraid to disobey.
At night it stood at the top of the long stairs
just to hear her talking.

The mask I swore my mother wore:

Small clouds like lace
on the brow. Eyepieces

I couldn't see through.
Even her small shoulders
would make me cry. When she died
I saw her face.

The mask I passed on to my children:

Comes late for dinner
and leaves early, clears the dishes quickly.
This mask
is all relatives alive or dead,
drunk, sober, or beautiful. Oh God, yes,
at least beautiful.
Everyone at the table finds a window,
stares intently through.

First Breast

A man sits on a chair's edge.
A nude woman stands facing him,
green towel around her hips,
the reach of her spine

sharp as a clean white bone.
He gazes at the shadow of her breast
as if for the first time
he will slip pale areola

between palate and tongue,
like a calf or a lamb
suckling with gratitude.
It is like a present;

he doesn't know what to do.
The breast moves toward him—
he leans forward
in his chair. It is wondrous

how calmly his lips open,
how quietly she watches
beyond the dark flint of his hair.
A white patch of neighborhood

fades outside the window frame;
trees poise silently, in breeze
light as breath against a woman's skin.
The unblessed nipple withers

in the chill evening air.
She is aware of the towel's restraint,
each loop rough against skin,
but warm. All these details.

To the Husband Who Stands at the Sink, Intent on Shaving

There is a woman in your shower,
her body visible through the green
canopy of steam. She isn't as young
as she used to be, but you've said
you hardly notice. Now her dark hair
cleaves to her neck like leaves
and beads of water decorate her skin,
slide opal and diamond bracelets down
the blood flush raised by heat.
Every day she walks or lifts weights,
praising the way thighs tighten,
how muscles rise and divide her back
into twin slices of fruit—sweet,
succulent, firm against the lip.
Now she admires the long arm she raises
to direct the spray against her breasts;
have you looked away from the mirror
to watch? In case you have, she turns,
giving you freely her profile, this map
of the body complete with betrayals
slightly hidden behind the wavering glass.
One hand ringed in gold
slowly approaches the faucet. Languid,
wide-awake, she prepares to emerge
like a water bird slipping from water
into air, feathers slicked, stripped clean
of anger and sorrow, not yet of expectation.

On the Wards

7 A.M. and all I can think of is sex,
sun just rising over the windowsill in waves,
a haze gathering over the Danbury skyline
that means a day hotter than hell. Could be
that argument we had this morning,
me slamming the door, all the things not said.

Usually the routine calms me—the bathing,
the bleached sheets, dark blue pills in their cups.
But the first patient today has angry breasts,
nipples big as my mother's thimbles.
Feeling suddenly like a child
who opens her mouth to rain, to lightning
burning down, I imagine
the unimaginable.

Then again, I never dared.
Even with the quiet ones in coma,
alone in the room when no one
would have known, the soft *hush hush*
of the respirator, their breasts crying out
from some awful memory, or the penis
lying half-dead over the lax thigh
and how it firms up, rising drunkenly.

I've never let my hands linger,
although I've wanted, just once, to look around
and, finding no one there, to raise the bed—
new sheets folded back over a body
carefully arranged, my stethoscope falling
from my neck, my stiff white blouse.

But how many breasts have I taken in my hands,
calling it "exam," and how many penises
betrayed me, enjoying their bath?—
and all those backs I've stroked, staring
at the walls beyond the patients' silhouettes,
coaxing them gently into sleep, safe
and guarded by my watch outside their door.

The Good Nurse

A good nurse kisses her patients
when she says good night.
—Elie Wiesel

Our kiss is in gratitude
for rumpled sheets, the hourly
turning of patients. For pillows
placed between legs,

cotton booties pulled over raw heels,
and in thanksgiving
for the patients' needs:
Their thirst quelled

by our cold glass.
Their pain,
sharp and relentless as a bee
charmed by our fingertips.

The kiss has everything to do
with sons who look at us
and disappear, daughters
who line their eyes with blue

and borrow our too-loud laughter.
We want to bind them
in our arms. Instead, we tend
the patient who longs for us.

He knows we will rush to him,
stroking his earlobe, kissing lightly
his eyelid, his cheek—
not for love,

but for what is constant:
the way skin hurries
to bruise, and the last gaze
freezes the mind.

How I Imagine It

Ahead of me on the road, my daughter
and her husband in their old Subaru.
He's driving and I'm following them to the Danbury garage
to fix the ping that's been there for weeks
when suddenly their car careens, crashes into a tree
and bursts into flames. I park my car, just stop it, and run,
run to the door bashed off its frame.
My hands reach in, carefully,
across her silky printed dress, the white-collared one
she likes so much. She is thin
and graceful, I unhook her seatbelt,
the silver metal clasp snaps open and the webbing falls away,
her head tilted as if she's sleeping,
but I smell gas, the stink of burning tires.
People cry out, shouting to me *Get away!* I lean in,
incredibly strong, and lift her up and out, she is all air,
long arms, hands with my knucklebones.
I hold her, wrap her dress around her knees,
her husband lies over the steering wheel, the horn blasting,
like in the movies, and I run, holding her in my arms.
I kneel by the roadside, let her body unfold
in a tree's green shadow, into long stems that smell like cut grass
the summers my father pushed the handmower and mother
made lemonade, squeezing the lemons in her hands, picking
each seed out. I bend,
knowing if I can save her, I can save myself, if I save her
she will forgive me for everything I have done,
for everything I have allowed to be done. I bend,
place my mouth over hers, take in one big breath, breathe it
into her mouth, into lungs that catch, grab it,
hurl it through to her heart, her heart
holds and contracts, once, again, again and she gasps for air.
I feel her warm, every cell ignites and glows, she is
alive. . . . The light
turns yellow, turns red. Their car slows ahead of me, stops.
The stoplight swings in the wind. It's almost Autumn.

Doctor, 8 P.M.

At dinner you speak of the tumor
you missed: A small spider

in the left upper lobe slipped
its net through vein and flesh to brain.

We eat in silence. All night you hold
X-rays up before an inner light.

Later, stretched white,
we love in the lightbulb's stare,

illumined like insects in a box.
Thrusting, thrusting, you note each flaw:

red blotch on my thigh,
my spider veins. Then we groan

and toss while silken lines
are stitched about our sleeping shapes

and drawn. We are bound by fears
we cannot loose, or satiate.

The Body Flute

O my body! I dare not desert
the likes of you in other
men and women, nor
the likes of the parts of you.
—Walt Whitman

I go on loving the flesh
after you die.
I close your eyes
bathe your bruised limbs
press down the edges of tape
sealing your dry wounds.

I walk with you to the morgue
and pillow your head
against the metal drawer. To me
this is your final resting place.
Your time with me
is the sum of your life.

I have met your husbands and wives
but I know who loved you most,
who owned the sum
of your visible parts.
The doctor and his theory
never owned you.

Nor did "medicine" or "hospital"
ever own you.
Couldn't you, didn't you
refuse tests, refuse to take your medicine?
But I am the nurse
of childhood's sounds in the night,

nurse of the washrag's sting
nurse of needle and sleep
nurse of lotion and hands on skin
nurse of sheets and nightmares
nurse of the flashlight beam at 3 A.M.

I know the privacy of vagina and rectum
I slip catheters into openings
I clean you like a mother does.

That which you allow no one,
you allow me.

✱

Who sat with you that night?
Your doctor was asleep,

your husband was driving in.
Your wife took a few things

home to wash, poor timing,
but she had been by your side for days.

Your kids? They could be anywhere,
even out with the vending machines

working out just how much
you did or didn't do for them.

✱

You waited
until you were alone
with me. You trusted

that I could wait and not be
frightened away.
That I would not expect

anything of you—
not bravery or anger, not even
a good fight.

At death
you become wholly mine.

☎

Your last glance, your last
sensation of touch,
your breath

I inhale, incorporating you
into memory.
Your body

silvery and still on the bed,
your lips fluttering into blue.
I pull your hand away from mine.

My other hand lingers, traces
your finger from the knucklebone
to the sheets

into which your body sinks,
my lips over yours,
my cheek near the blue

absence of your breath,
my hands closing
the silver stops of your eyelids.

Cloudburst

All the green witches
are tossing their hair. The wind

is a priest with a harsh voice
and there is one black crow

in the tulip tree, bracing himself
among broad leaves. His presence

reminds me of death,
his mouth hard and half-open,

like someone dying, not quite
a corpse. The fuchsia

is beaten like an old woman
attacked in her apartment. Rain

coils its tongue along Umpawaug Road
and lightning electrocutes the sky.

Voices shout. Thunder rattles its tin plate,
doors and gates clang shut.

Now I watch as the sun in the distance,
like a soft-shod nurse,

hurries to cluck over the damage,
shaking her bright bandage scissors.

About the Author

Cortney Davis, a nurse practitioner, is the author of *The Body Flute*, a chapbook from Adastra Press (1994), and co-editor of an anthology, *Between the Heartbeats: Poetry and Prose by Nurses* (University of Iowa Press, 1995). Her poems have been published in *CALYX Journal, Crazyhorse, The Hudson Review, Literature and Medicine, Ms., Poetry East, Poet & Critic, The Journal of the American Medical Association, Pivot, Yankee*, and other journals.

Davis is the recipient of an NEA poetry fellowship and two Connecticut Commission on the Arts poetry grants. Honors include the Anna Davidson Rosenberg Award in Poetry from the Judah Magnes Museum in California.

Davis holds a BA and MA in English in addition to her nursing credentials. She lives in Redding, CT, and works as a nurse practitioner in women's health.

"Eventually, nursing and poetry merge: a perfect place in which the act of caring becomes a way of keeping, and the mysteries of our world are revealed in the sensual reality of physical detail." —Cortney Davis.

Selected Titles from Award-Winning CALYX Books

NONFICTION

Natalie on the Street by Ann Nietzke. A day-by-day account of the author's relationship with an elderly homeless woman who lived on the streets of Nietzke's central Los Angeles neighborhood. *PEN West Finalist.*
ISBN 0-934971-41-2, $14.95, paper; ISBN 0-934971-42-0, $24.95, cloth.

The Violet Shyness of Their Eyes: Notes from Nepal by Barbara J. Scot. A moving account of a western woman's transformative sojourn in Nepal as she reaches mid-life. *PNBA Book Award.*
ISBN 0-934971-35-8, $14.95, paper; ISBN 0-934971-36-6, $24.95, cloth.

In China with Harpo and Karl by Sibyl James. Essays revealing a feminist poet's experiences while teaching in Shanghai, China.
ISBN 0-934971-15-3, $9.95, paper; ISBN 0-934971-16-1, $17.95, cloth.

FICTION

Second Sight by Rickey Gard Diamond. This debut novel is a chilling portrait of one family's complicated and violent interactions. *"Invites comparison to Margaret Atwood's* Surfacing...." — Molly Gloss
ISBN 0-934971-55-2, $14.95, paper; ISBN 0-934971-56-0, $28.95, cloth.

Four Figures in Time by Patricia Grossman. This novel tracks the lives of four characters in a New York art school. Here the rarefied world of making art meets the mundane world of making ends meet.
ISBN 0-934971-47-1, $13.95, paper; ISBN 0-934971-48-X, $25.95, cloth.

The Adventures of Mona Pinsky by Harriet Ziskin. In this fantastical novel, a 65-year-old Jewish woman, facing alienation and ridicule, comes of age and ultimately is reborn on a heroine's journey.
ISBN 0-934971-43-9, $12.95, paper; ISBN 0-934971-44-7, $24.95, cloth.

Killing Color by Charlotte Watson Sherman. These compelling, mythical short stories by a gifted storyteller explore the African-American experience. *Washington Governor's Award.*
ISBN 0-934971-17-X, $9.95, paper; ISBN 0-934971-18-8, $19.95, cloth.

Mrs. Vargas and the Dead Naturalist by Kathleen Alcalá. Fourteen stories set in Mexico and the Southwestern U.S., written in the tradition of magical realism.
ISBN 0-934971-25-0, $9.95, paper; ISBN 0-934971-26-9, $19.95, cloth.

Ginseng and Other Tales from Manila by Marianne Villanueva. Poignant short stories set in the Philippines. *Manila Critic's Circle National Literary Award Nominee.*
ISBN 0-934971-19-6, $9.95, paper; ISBN 0-934971-20-X, $19.95, cloth.

POETRY

Another Spring, Darkness: Selected Poems of Anuradha Mahapatra translated by Carolyne Wright, et al. The first English translation of poetry by this working-class woman from West Bengal. *"These are burning poems, giving off a spell of light...."*—Linda Hogan
ISBN 0-934971-51-X, $12.95 paper; ISBN 0-934971-52-8, $23.95, cloth.

The Country of Women by Sandra Kohler. A collection of poetry that explores a woman's experience as sexual being, as mother, as artist. Kohler finds art in the mundane, the sacred, and the profane.
ISBN 0-934971-45-5, $11.95, paper; ISBN 0-934971-46-3, $21.95, cloth.

Light in the Crevice Never Seen by Haunani-Kay Trask. This first book of poetry by an indigenous Hawaiian to be published in North America is about a Native woman's love for her land, and the inconsolable grief and rage that come from its destruction.
ISBN 0-934971-37-4, $11.95, paper; ISBN 0-934971-38-2, $21.95, cloth.

Open Heart by Judith Mickel Sornberger. An elegant collection of poetry rooted in a woman's relationships with family, ancestors, and the world.
ISBN 0-934971-31-5, $9.95, paper; ISBN 0-934971-32-3, $19.95, cloth.

Raising the Tents by Frances Payne Adler. A personal and political volume of poetry, documenting a Jewish woman's discovery of her voice.
ISBN 0-934971-33-1, $9.95, paper; ISBN 0-934971-34-X, $19.95, cloth.

Black Candle: Poems about Women from India, Pakistan, and Bangladesh by Chitra Divakaruni. Lyrical and honest poems that chronicle significant moments in the lives of South Asian women. *Gerbode Award*.
ISBN 0-934971-23-4, $9.95, paper; ISBN 0-934971-24-2, $19.95 cloth.

Indian Singing in 20th Century America by Gail Tremblay. A brilliant work of hope by a Native American poet.
ISBN 0-934971-13-7, $9.95, paper; ISBN 0-934971-14-5, $19.95, cloth.

Idleness Is the Root of All Love by Christa Reinig, translated by Ilze Mueller. These poems by the prize-winning German poet accompany two older lesbians through a year in love and struggle.
ISBN 0-934971-21-8, $10, paper; ISBN 0-934971-22-6, $18.95, cloth.

ANTHOLOGIES

Present Tense: Writing and Art by Young Women edited by Micki Reaman and the CALYX young women's editorial collective. This groundbreaking anthology of original work by women who have come of age during CALYX's lifetime is a glimpse into the future generation of feminist literature and art.
ISBN 0-934971-53-6, $14.95, paper; ISBN 0-934971-54-4, $26.95, cloth.

The Forbidden Stitch: An Asian American Women's Anthology edited by Shirley Geok-lin Lim, et al. The first Asian American women's anthology. *American Book Award.*
ISBN 0-934971-04-8, $16.95, paper; ISBN 0-934971-10-2, $32, cloth.

Women and Aging, An Anthology by Women edited by Jo Alexander, et al. The only anthology that addresses ageism from a feminist perspective. A rich collection of older women's voices.
ISBN 0-934971-00-5, $15.95, paper; ISBN 0-934971-07-2, $28.95, cloth.

The International Anthology. A stunning dual-language anthology of translated work by women from twenty countries. Spanning centuries and the world, it features poetry by 1996 Nobel Laureate Wislawa Szymborska (translated by Grazyna Drabik and Sharon Olds). *"Extraordinary...awesome how such a span of time and place has been made in a single volume..."* William Pitt Root, *Small Press Review*
ISBN 0-934971-59-5, $12, paper

CALYX Books are available to the trade from Consortium and other major distributors and jobbers.

Individuals may order direct from

CALYX Books
P.O. Box B
Corvallis, OR 97339

Send check or money order in U.S. currency; add $3.00 shipping and handling for the first book, $1.00 for each additional book.
*Credit card orders only: **FAX** to 541-753-0515*
*or call toll-free **1-888-FEM BOOK***

CALYX, A Journal of Art and Literature by Women

CALYX, A Journal of Art and Literature by Women, has showcased the work of over two thousand women artists and writers since 1976. Committed to providing a forum for *all* women's voices, *CALYX* presents diverse styles, images, issues, and themes which women writers and artists are exploring.

CALYX holds a special place in my heart. Some of my very first published words—two poems—were published in CALYX years ago. I've never forgotten the thrill of turning those beautifully illustrated pages and seeing my name, my earnest words, *printed there alongside those of some of my literary heroines. It made me feel as if I belonged to the important company of women.*
— Barbara Kingsolver

The work you do brings dignity, intelligence, and a sense of wholeness to the world. I am only one of many who bows respectfully— to all of you and to your work.

—Barry Lopez

Published twice a year, Summer and Winter; three issues per volume.
CALYX Journal is available to the trade from Ingram Periodicals and other major distributors.
CALYX Journal is available at your local bookstore or direct from:

CALYX, Inc.
P.O. Box B
Corvallis, OR 97339

CALYX is committed to producing books of literary, social, and feminist integrity.

CALYX, Inc., is a nonprofit organization with a 501(C)(3) status. All donations are tax deductible.

Colophon

The text of this book was composed in Cheltenham Light
with titles in Stuyvesant Solid.
Page layout and composition provided by
ImPrint Services, Corvallis, Oregon.

Dr. Richard Selzer

Lewis Thomas chair @ cornell